We Learn Something Everyday

Nature's Wonders – We Learn Something Everyday

D. M. Chatwin

Paper Doll

© D. M. Chatwin 1999

Published by Paper Doll
Belasis Hall
Coxwold Way
Billingham
Cleveland

ISBN: 1 86248 117 2

Typeset by CBS, Martlesham Heath,
Ipswich, Suffolk
Printed by Lintons Printers, Co. Durham

Dedication

Lesley Temple, a very dear friend for many years, who had faith in me and encouraged me to achieve a place in life, she died in 1989 aged 102.

CONTENTS

'Dickensia' (I)	1
'Dickensia' (II)	3
The Visit	5
Christmas Day	7
Hope (I)	9
Clouds	11
My Tree	12
Continuo	14
Raindrops	15
Hope (II)	16
Memories	17
My Friend	19
March The First	21
Perseverance	22
Love Leads The Way	23
Natural Trust	26
'Strawberry Fayre'	28
John	30
Dennis	33
Dawn	35
The Sycamore Tree	37
Fairies	40
Deception	42
Life Goes On	44
Hope (III)	46
Friends	47
Consolation	49
A Modern Miracle	50

'DICKENSIA' (I)

Have you ever lived in 'Dickensia'?
I have, long years ago.
I went to teach in a boarding school
Up north where all was cold.

I shared a room with another girl
Who was only filling in time,
Till she was of age to train as a nurse,
A role which would suit her fine.

Our hearts sank low when we saw our room,
Bare boards all stained with brown.
A single rug beside each bed
Worth naught but a couple of pounds!

A chest of drawers stood beside each bed
And what was that other queer thing?
An enamel dish with a funnel of red,
A candle! – that made me cringe.

The following nights were cold downstairs
So we went to bed to read.
The only light from the candle's glare
Met our immediate need.

By the end of the week there was little left.
What had we better do?
We went to the kitchen and there was the 'Head',
'Well! What can I do for you?'

'A candle please, for ours are burnt out
And no way can we see.'
What *do* you girls do?' she said with a shout,
'That candle should last you a week!'

We left with our spoils and we hatched a plot
Whereby we could foil 'the dragon'
Next day after school we went to the shops
And bought two pounds of candles!

Then every night for the rest of our stay
We undressed by the light of 'can – one'
Then switched to 'can – two' and shouted hooray
As we settled to read! For we'd won!

'DICKENSIA' (II)

We didn't have a staffroom, we had to use the classroom
And one armchair was shared between we three.
The fire was low and chilly like an atmospheric tomb
And only coke left now with which to feed!

The boarders did their homework in a room below our floor,
Where all was warm and cosy with a fire.
A scuttle full of coal stood in the hearth quite near the door
If only we could have that coal up higher!

We three took turns to supervise the boarders and their prep
And secretly went down before they came.
We wrapped some coal in paper and stealthily we crept
And hid it in a cupboard with the cane!

When all the class was settled and working very hard
As quiet as mice we ran up with the coal
And gave it to our colleagues both huddled by the hearth
Relieved to know that we had reached our goal!

The atmosphere got worse as the weeks and
   months went by.
We two decided we must leave this place.
Sarcastic language reigned which often made me
   cry.
To teach there longer seemed an utter waste.

The following week we 'bearded the lioness in
   her den'.
With fear and trembling gave our notice in.
To our surprise she accepted with no sarcastic
   gems.
The final curtain fell with only 'FIN'!

THE VISIT

I have a big black spider who comes to visit me.
As soon as Autumn chill occurs he asks himself to tea!

He runs across the carpet on his tiny stilted legs,
Examines all the furniture before coming to me next!

With anxious fear I dodge him and jump out of my chair.
He zigzags back and forth again then disappears from there.

The following day I saw him as he ran across the floor
Full steam ahead to the bathroom, then escaped behind the door.

The next two days were peaceful, no sign of him at all.
I wondered where he'd got to? Asleep behind a wall?

Quite early the next morning in the kitchen by the sink
I saw my friendly spider by the plughole – having a drink.

I covered him with the dishcloth and picked him
    up right quick
Then dropped him on the kitchen floor where he
    ran behind the fridge.

This spider liked my little house, I began to feel
    quite friendly
And wondered next where would we meet for I
    knew I'd treat him gently!

The time had come to change the towels. I choose
    the colour blue.
I turned my head to hang them up – Alas! he was
    floating in the loo!

CHRISTMAS DAY

I didn't have a Christmas tree to adorn my little home
But I had a fluffy fern just four feet high.
It stood upon a table in the corner of the room
Its fronds cascading high and low and wide.

I draped the lights round picture frames in the angle of the wall,
Then twined them in the fern's fine pointed leaves.
Small bells were hung on either side of the plant's secure supports
Then model birds were brought to their new tree.

A tinsel star with a bird each side was fastened to the top
And twinkling bells rang out ding dong ding dong.
I put my model tawny owl to sit within the pot
And imagined all the birds in joyous song.

The morning light was pale and grey, the room was steely blue.
The fairy lights tried hard to shine their best.
I had to watch the daylight fade which lowered all the hues
Before the lights could shine out strong and fresh.

By four o'clock my lovely tree sent forth its warming glow
Of globes of light with red, blue, green and yellow on the wall.
The Star shone bright like days of yore touching many souls.
It could have been the Damascus Road where Jesus met St Paul.

HOPE (I)

I opened my curtains one wintry morn
The scene was cold and bleak.
The trees were like skeletons ragged and torn
And black leaves waved high out of reach.

A solitary blackbird bounced in a bush
Hoping a breakfast to find.
He snatched at odd berries which he hastily crushed
Then flew off to rest in the pines.

As I looked at the windows with curtains all drawn
The houses were looking quite dead.
I wondered what sounds woke folk up in the morn
To get them all out of their beds!

As I stood musing, depression increased,
I wondered if life was worthwhile.
Then suddenly low in the sky t'wards the east
The clouds opened up and spread wide.

They gracefully broke into wonderful shapes,
Revealing marvellous colours between.
One space was filled like an azure lake
With streaks of gold and green.

As the sun pushed its way to greet the day,
Gay heralds announced its power,
With pennants of yellow and pink displayed
At this wonderful morning hour.

Higher and higher rose the sun
Flooding the world with light,
The clouds dispersed into fluffy balls
Tinged with red and white.

The wonder of watching that beautiful scene
Strengthened my will to cope.
We can't live on memories of what has been
But resolve to be strong and hope.

CLOUDS

What a joy it can be to lie in the sun
And gaze at the sky so blue.
It isn't long before interesting shapes
Come floating by to you.

Look at that beautiful cotton wool mound
As soft as a baby's bed.
I could jump into that with one bound
And sleep soundly for years ahead!

A flock of sheep follows close behind.
Each lit by a golden light
From the sinking sun way out to the west
Announcing the herald of night.

But not yet please, for behind that tree
Another mass is forming.
What have we here, tall turrets three,
A castle with ominous warning.

Is a fairy princess imprisoned in there?
Will her prince arrive in time?
I'm not sure I can handle this thought just now
For the sun says there isn't much time.

And so it goes on, these valleys and peaks
Of imagery in the air;
But you can't hold on to deceptive sight
Of things that are not really there!

MY TREE

I rescued a sycamore seedling
From the roots of my garden hedge
And planted it new in a six inch pot
Surrounded with rich soil instead.

As the years passed by it grew straight and tall
Till it filled a ten inch container.
My garden's too small to plant such a tree
And not enough soil to maintain it.

What could I do to help my tree?
I couldn't now desert it.
Then one fine day a friend said to me
'Why don't you try and transport it?'

Now who would want a sycamore tree
That grows to thirty feet or more?
'I know just the place,' she said to me
'An old people's Home. I live next door.'

I sought out this Home and discovered it planned
To make an enclosed garden
For all the residents to enjoy
In the eve of their late retirement.

The Prince's Trust was involved in this
And gifts came from everywhere.
My tree was accepted. I made a strong wish
That the site would be right and fair.

Autumn, Winter, and Spring passed by
My tree survived them all.
Bright green shoots stretched their tips on high
Ready prepared for next 'fall'.

Then one sad day I looked for my tree
And it was no longer there.
The management had decided 'en masse'
It should be replanted elsewhere.

But where was it now I wanted to know?
Enquiries drew a blank.
Apologies filtered throughout the Home
My thoughts and heart just sank.

Enquiries continued throughout the next week
And I called again to enquire
What had happened to my beloved tree.
Its welfare my main desire.

A member of staff had taken it home
To her village a few miles away
And planted it firmly in a new garden plot
Where it could spread its branches each day.

She promised to send me a picture one day
To show how it was progressing.
As long as it's safe in a loving home
There's no need for me to be fretting!

CONTINUO

The gay laburnum shook its tassels in the bright
    and breezy air.
Its golden florets full of pollen attracted bees
    from everywhere;
But all too soon their colour faded; tassels
    showed the signs of wear.
The fragile petals lost their colour and each
    looked like a man's grey beard!

Catoneaster standing by, said, 'Don't give up all
    hope as yet.
Just look at my firm heads of cream which shine
    with light towards the west.
Too soon a change will come to me, my flowers
    will turn to brown;
But in the Autumn days to come I'll wear a
    flaming crown!'

The dainty blackberry by the wall stretched up
    its prickly stalks.
Its pinky petals open wide to receive all nature's
    thoughts.
The changes that take place each day in nature's
    garden fair,
Tell us there is no death, but life to come, as year
    succeeds to year.

RAINDROPS

Have you ever watched the raindrops running
    down the window pane?
They chase each other all the way, as if they're
    playing games.
The game of 'Touch' it seems to me is what they
    try to do
Just like we played at break time when we were
    all at school.

But they are far too clever as they zigzag down
    the pane.
They have an unseen helper – the breeze – that
    guides their games.
No winner in their race I see as they make their
    way straight down,
'Hello there! Watch me run and try to catch me if
    you can.'

The cloud has passed, the sun comes out, the
    drops are forced to rest.
Each one shines bright with twinkling stars just
    like an evening dress.
The sun shines long and warms the glass, the
    droplets disappear.
Ah well! My window's nice and clean. You've
    'touched' my heart you dears!

HOPE (II)

The winter sky is dark and grey
With anguish fear and sorrow.
The fierce winds blow across the world.
There is no sweet tomorrow.

On on across the frozen earth
Of heartless cruelty
You have no strength to beat the foe
Of cold adversity.

But . . . softly from behind those clouds
The warmth of love is stealing
And soft spring rains burst through the clouds
And drench the world with healing.

MEMORIES

'The Walks' at King's Lynn was my favourite
    haunt
When I was a carefree child.
I skipped through its paths on my way to school
With thoughts both gay and wild.

My special path I called 'The Bumps'
Of miniature 'hills' and 'dales'.
Afforded such fun as I skipped along
Up and down and between the 'vales'.

It bordered allotments from end to end
In sight of the railway track.
Where shunting took place nearly every day
With a noisy clickerty – clack.

On my way home on the other side
Was grass and a lily pond.
My friend and I sang as we ran along
Me swinging my hat round and round.

The elastic broke, hat flew in the air
And landed in the pond!
My friend Eric Bell with practical skill
Hooked it out with great aplomb.

We raced for home, my Gran was there.
She grabbed two pegs and ran.
She hung it on the garden line
As Mum came in with the pram.

What happened next I can't recall.
My fears were quite unfounded.
The 'Walks' and pond I'll always love.
For happy thoughts surround it.

MY FRIEND

The last rose of summer stood straight and tall,
Its bud tightly closed against the cold.
From my window I watched it uncurl
Its delicate petals the texture of pearls.

This bush was always a favourite with me.
I admired its tenacious attempts to be free.
Neither cold wind or rain stopped its progress in time.
Each morning I looked for the opening sign!

Ah! Yes! there it was, day two showed a break
In the calyx green sheath. The flower was awake!
It twisted and turned throughout the long day.
The first pink petal has come to stay.

The way was now clear for others to follow.
What would I see from my window tomorrow?
The darkness hid my friend from sight,
So I pulled the curtains and wished her, 'Goodnight!'

The following morning was clear and bright.
I flung back the curtains to let in the light.
My rose was now free from her sepal's protection
And stood firm like a candle in all her perfection.

Two weeks of joy were ours each day
As we smiled at each other and I begged her to stay.
But time is relentless and knocks us about,
My dear rose did suffer great loss there's no doubt.

At the end of three weeks there was one petal left.
It was stronger and fairer than all the rest.
With sadness I watched as she tugged herself free
And I knew in my heart she'd waved 'Goodbye' to me.

MARCH THE FIRST

March the first dawned bright and clear,
On the crisp and frosty air.
Larks sang blithely in the blue
Singing songs of hope anew.
The sad laburnum hung its head
With tears of ice hard pressed to check.
The pyracantha defied the cold
And shone with diamonds bright and bold.
'I'm here beside my friend the tree
To guard her from the winter freeze.'
'And so am I,' the crisp grass said.
'I shield her feet, you guard her head.'
In the dykes the ice did melt,
For the touch of Spring was felt.
O'er the fields of sparkling snow,
The sun said warmly, 'You must go!
Your work is done upon the earth,
Away! and let the flowers give birth!'

PERSEVERANCE

Mother blackbird watched her fledgling
Perch upon the water tray.
Her beak was full of tasty food.
She hoped he would not stray.

She caressed his beak with the dainty morsel;
But he wasn't ready to eat.
He moved away from her loving advances
And beat a hasty retreat.

She waited till he returned to his seat
And flopped into the water.
With quiet persistence she opened his beak
And he no longer fought her.

Mum watched him calmly hold it tight,
Defiant and quite cool;
But – 'No – I'll not give up the fight!'
And he dropped it in the pool!

Patient Mum was not deterred.
She jumped into the dish.
Whipped out the piece of precious food
And off she flew with it!!

LOVE LEADS THE WAY

'Nobody wants me,' the little cat sighed.
As she was chased into the kitchen.
Her only place was a hard upright chair
With a threadbare mat to sit on.

When Spring burst through the leaden sky
She decided to run away.
She sniffed her way to the privet hedge
And enjoyed a lovely day.

For through the hedge she spied a house
All sparkling clear and bright
She slowly crept towards the door,
As no one was in sight.

The house said, 'Welcome little one.
Why not come inside?
Here's a cardboard box for you.
Jump up and you can hide.'

With one light spring she gained the shelf
And sniffed all round the box.
Then stepped inside and curled up small
And slept till four o'clock!

Just then a voice was heard to say,
'Hello! What have we here?'
Then puss looked up with frightened eyes
Her body full of fear.

A gentle hand came slowly down
And stroked her silky fur.
'It's alright love, you're safe with me
Just show me how you purr!'

Every day she made her way
To the cosy house of glass
She curled up small and slept for hours
And soon forgot her past!

When Autumn came and chill winds blew
She had to think again.
'I'll try the red brick house this time
To shelter from the rain.'

She lightly stepped across the lawn
And waited at the door.
A figure moved behind the glass
She wondered more and more.

At last the door was opened wide.
She sensed a cosy room.
'Come in my little furry friend
Enjoy your nice new home!'

'Patchie', a tortoiseshell Manx cat arrived in the neighbourhood because of a divorce. Her owner came home to 'Mum', who did not like cats and was very houseproud; hence banishment to the kitchen. Eventually I was allowed to have her permanently. She lived with me till she died aged seventeen years. She was a lovely natured animal and deserved a good home.

NATURAL TRUST

The blackberry bush, now full in flower
Stretched wide its petals to the sun,
And as I watched in this magic hour
A bumble bee soft to the petals clung.

So peaceful he looked as he nestled there
With his brown velvet coat so neat and trim.
I stroked his back with never a fear.
My heart filled with love for this tiny thing.

'You're not really safe to stay there till dawn.
The petals may fall before the night.
Please move to a safer place by morn
Then gently leave with the early light.'

It was now eight o'clock and the air was cool
As I made my way back to the blackberry bush.
But . . . where was my friend, so like a brown jewel?
Curled round a firm bud, fast asleep . . . hush!

The following morn as the clock struck eight,
I tripped down the garden path.
My friend was still there in sleepy state
Enjoying dreams of his past.

At eleven o'clock I retraced my steps
To have a look at my bee;
But when I got there he had quietly left –
He had work to do like me!

I was glad to know he was safe that night.
God's creatures instinctively trust.
He knew that bud was a safer site
For he felt Love's tender touch.

I was fascinated, watching this bee snugly clinging to the open flower. He was so secure. He didn't move when I stroked him. I was also curious to see how long he would stay; hence my watchfulness. Watching nature can be very enlightening. It moves by inner instinct not reason like we do!

'STRAWBERRY FAYRE'

The Greengrocer's shop in Norfolk Street
Was full of delightful smells.
My mother made jam in strawberry time
And stacked all the jars on our shelves.

The man in the shop pushed the fruit in a scoop
And filled a large bag to the top.
I helped my mother carry the load
And smiling, we left the shop.

The berries were washed when we got back home
And large fruit sorted for tea.
'I must go to the shop across the road.'
My mother said to me.

'Look after Estelle, I shan't be long
You can begin to set the table.
If you've the time to spare while I am gone
Please write 'strawberry' on these labels.'

The tang of the fruit became a desire.
Into the pantry I walked.
I took two, then four, then six -
Oh my! What do I do with the stalks?

Into the garden I quickly fled
And buried them in the soil.
My mother returned and nothing was said.
I relaxed in my mind for a while.

Two weeks went by, my Dad's letter arrived
For he was away in the forces.
His letters contained a pen and ink sketch
Based on the pranks of his daughter!

This one showed me crouched down on my knees
Planting stalks in the soil of the border!
I glanced at my Mum with fear in my heart
But she smiled at her bungling daughter!

'How did you know?' I shakily asked.
For no one else could have told her.
'The soil was hard and hot from the sun
But your patch was loose and much colder!'

I believe I still have the sketch my Dad drew
among my archives!

JOHN

I loved my John with the shining eyes,
His loneliness tore at my heart.
He came to the 'Home' with no one to care,
His family torn apart.

We did our best to make up to him
When others were taken out.
His health was frail, his back was weak,
To walk was much in doubt.

A chair was found to cover the ground
Of miles of country lanes.
We laughed and joked as we sailed along,
Love helped to relieve his pain.

Months advanced, the T.B. spread.
He bore it all with some tears.
'Oh hold my hand,' he cried one day,
'Your presence shows you care.'

His fight for life continued.
The flame was small and dim.
He slept for hours, exhausted.
The future looked so grim.

School term ended quickly.
The time for a needed break.
The urge to stay possessed me;
But leave I had to take.

Nurse said, 'Now go, you cannot stay
He might linger here for weeks
And you'll return a brighter ray
To help him gain relief.'

At sixteen years it seemed unfair,
That such a life should fail.
What had he done to deserve all this
Since coming to the Dales?

My heart was sad throughout the week.
I held him in my mind.
I longed to return to 'Hollins Hall'
To help him try to smile.

Then one fine day, the sky was clear.
The swallows flying high.
At one o'clock John 'spoke' to me
And whispered with a sigh.

'It's lovely here. I'm happy now.
So happy I can see.'
A subtle calm stole over me.
Rejoice, O Lord. He's free.

The following day a message came
From Matron of the Home.
'Just thought you'd like to know the end.
John passed away at noon.'

This happened when I taught at a Barnardo Hospital Home in Yorkshire 1940-50. It's a long story. He was one of eight children; all eventually taken into care because mother could not cope through illness. John was awarded the Scouts V.C. for his bravery. Scouts carried his coffin into the church on the day of burial.

DENNIS

At the age of fifteen I had two younger sisters
But always longed for a brother.
To my great delight as the months flew by
A son was born to my mother.

Alas, his form was very weak
He had no urge for food.
One day Mum placed him in my arms
And softly left the room.

I rocked him gently and kissed his sweet face,
My tears began to flow.
'Oh, please God, no, don't call him home yet.
We can't face that dreadful blow!'

He stirred in my arms and opened his eyes
And fixed them fully on mine
Then stretched out stiff with a gentle sigh,
His dear little face looked divine.

My mother returned with some warm baby food.
Stopped short as she gazed on the scene.
'He's gone,' she said, her voice full of tears
'An angel on earth he has been.'

Later that day he was laid to rest
In a coffin of plain white wood
Encircled with sweet smelling lilies
And we kissed him goodbye where we stood.

An aunt of mine came, to pay her respects,
And I showed her into the room.
She had one carnation in her hand
A pink and perfect bloom.

As she gazed at my brother's face
Her eyes glazed with frozen tears,
She gently placed the flower in his hands
And kissed his golden hair.

I'll never forget that dear baby
Though many a year has passed by.
His presence is ever with me.
We'll meet again with great joy.

DAWN

The garden lawn was sparkling with myriad drops of dew
All shining with the spectrum's varied lights.
Each blade stood straight and turgid with red and green and blue.
Displaying diamonds, brilliant to the sight.

Dawn spread across the clear blue sky and birds began to sing.
I stroked the blackbird sitting in its nest.
She didn't move, but stared at me and spread her loving wings.
'No harm will come to you my dear, just settle there and rest.'

I listened to my garden in the dawn's early light
And heard a rustling underneath the hedge.
A hedgehog scuttled by and disappeared from sight.
I guessed she was off to seek her bed!

The flowers unfurled their beauty and opened to the sky,
And bees began their tireless daily round
Of seeking nectar sweet where'er they flew on high
And brought it to the hives upon the ground.

The beauty of the garden in the hour of early
    light
Is near to God's perfection ever seen.
For ONE IS ALL and ALL IS ONE within His
    perfect sight.
His sparkling beauty there for all to see.

THE SYCAMORE TREE

A sycamore seedling spiralled to earth
And got caught in the privet hedge.
It hung there for hours from the time of its birth,
'Please find me a warm secure ledge.'

The air grew cooler as the sun went down
But the breeze was kind at heart.
It gave one strong puff and pushed it around,
The seed stabbed the earth like a dart!

'Oh thank you breeze,' said the little seed
'Now I'll be warm and cosy.
I'll push down my roots and tuck myself in
For all is secure and rosy.'

The following spring awoke the seed
And it soon began to grow.
It stretched its stem to be one foot high
And happily swung to and fro.

But not for long did the tiny tree
Enjoy its home in the hedge,
For one fine day it screamed with pain
As its roots were torn from its ledge.

'Oh where am I going?' he cried with fear.
As he felt himself carried along.
For kind human hands, active quite near
Were trying to right a wrong!

The tree's tiny roots were gently placed
In a pot of pliable soil.
'Oh this is good. I can spread myself.
My life is no longer a toil.'

Years passed by, the tree grew so tall
And changed 'homes' several times.
It stood six feet high beside a wall,
But longed to feel the sunshine.

Then once again it was carried away
'Oh where am I going now?
At least my roots are safe today
And something is laying me down!'

With a bang of a door and a mighty roar
The tree felt itself on the move.
Propelled along as it lay on the floor
Scared stiff as it rolled to and fro.

It didn't take long as the distance was short
And the tree was lifted free.
Within the hour it was safe in port
The tree had all its needs.

'Oh this is fine,' the sycamore said,
'I have light, shade, sun and rain
And plenty of space to spread my leaves
And the birds are becoming quite tame.'

But once again it suffered a shock
When forks and spades and knives
Began hacking away at its roots below
And made a gash in its stock.

Its roots were wrenched out and wrapped in a sack
And the tree was dumped in a van
Which rumbled along a bumpy track
Then came to stop on green land.

Once more the tree was lifted out
And planted in a deep hole.
Soft soil was sprinkled round its roots
Which made them nice and cool.

The fears of the tree were nearly gone
As it gazed upon the scene
Of a carpet of green with bushes and pond
And in the distance a stream.

The tree felt a tickle amongst its twigs
And parting its leaves to see –
'Hello little bird. You're not very big
Come and make friends with me.'

FAIRIES

'Do you believe in fairies?'
My young friend said to me.
'Oh yes,' I said, 'I've seen them
Dancing in a field.'

How well I remember that evening
When I was just ten years old.
I'd made sure the rabbits were feeding
Then ran through the gate to the road.

I climbed a stile and skipped along
Between rows and rows of peas.
The dainty scent from their tiny flowers
Attracted the swarming of bees.

At the end of this plot was a blackberry hedge
And beyond it a lovely green field.
I knew my way through by a secret ledge
Hidden behind an oak tree.

The air was still as the sun went down
And gentle sounds could be heard.
The swish of insects twirling around
And the goodnight song of the birds.

I watched all this as I crouched by the tree.
I was one with this new found world.
My heart and mind were completely free
Like a ship with its sail unfurled.

The sun had gone, the wood was like night.
A mist had begun to form;
But there at my feet was a ring of light.
My circle of fairies was born!

They danced around in this magic ring
Their bodies sparkling with dew.
My joy was supreme when they began to sing
The excitement grew and grew.

They leapt in the air like shooting stars
Then glided gracefully down
And huddled together among the long grass
Then disappeared underground!

You may not believe this dainty tale
Of happiness taking shape – but -
Why shouldn't we peep behind the veil
To see what's there – while we wait?!

DECEPTION

The air was warm, the sky was blue.
Butterflies hovered in every hue.
The dainty white with tips of black,
The ornate peacock with 'eyes' on its back.

Ah, what is that one settling there
With wings outstretched with never a care?
Patches of yellow, orange and black,
Crescents of blue which always match.

This tortoiseshell small is prettiest of all
As he basks in the sun against the wall.
But wait – what is that I hear in the distance
Rumbles of thunder, low and persistent.

Raindrops splash and dance in the breeze.
The tortoiseshell flutters away with ease.
He makes for a fence with an overhang top
And with wings tightly folded, there he stops.

Protected safely from splashes of rain,
I hasten indoors to do the same.
A cup of tea would be most refreshing,
Than 'tortie' and I would both be resting!

The storm has passed, the clouds dispersed
I wandered outside expecting the worst.
I couldn't see my beautiful friend
Just a rusty long clamp in the fence's end.

But as I looked closer my vision cleared.
Not everything seems as it appears.
The rusty clamp attached to the boards
Was my tortoiseshell friend. I gazed in awe!

When danger is present Mother Nature protects
And guards her friends like a kindly hostess
With camouflage clever in every way
They live to see another day!

LIFE GOES ON

I watched a spray of roses
With buds from one to four
'Twas like a tiny posy
Seeking shelter from the storm.

The tall bud in the centre
With one on either side
Protected 'four' so tender
Its petals opening wide.

They succoured it with loving care
Its way through life to guide.
It faced the sun so warm and near
And then began to die.

The second bud its sepals spread
To give their friend support
'Four' tried to hard to lift its head
But the effort came to nought.

Friend 'three' was shorter and so strong
It spread its sepals wide
And hugged the rose with loving bonds
Close by her gentle side.

One by one the petals fell.
Its silent beauty gone.
The other two in peace could dwell
Enjoying June's sweet song.

And so like life the days pass by
Our friends support our needs.
Then suddenly we heave a sigh
And to new life we yield.

HOPE (III)

The stark laburnum twigs were bare
In the cold and frosty air.
The wiry tips all curved and black
Like witches' nails preparing to scratch.

But as the days of Spring drew near
The clearer hues of life appeared.
The juices of oncoming Spring
Softened twigs and everything.

Soon pendant tassels of fresh buds
Announced the promise of new life.
Never mind the blackest night.
In God's promise we must trust.

All will be well.

FRIENDS

I love my tall laburnum
As everybody knows,
I nurtured it across the years
Since it was six weeks old.

It lived in pots of varying size
Encouraged so to grow
Into a tree of five feet high
Its branches spreading low.

Its final place was in the soil
Beside my garden gate.
Now ten feet tall, its flowers right royal
It never knew its fate!

Then one sad day I looked outside
To wish it a 'Good morning'
It had split in half, trunk open wide
Its branches downward pouring.

I got a friend to clear the drive
Of overhanging branches.
I couldn't believe my tree had died
Which I with love had planted.

Its friend the pyracantha
Grew quietly by its side
But now its wish was granted
To be free and not to hide.

The space and air around it
Will encourage it to grow.
The bush's life had proved true grit
While living there below.

And so we see our own lives
With problems dark as night
Then suddenly the sun shines through
And clouds disperse from sight.

CONSOLATION

The emptiness of my little house was almost too much to bear.
The silence was like the grave.
I sat in the corner of my room with only a vacant stare.
I tried so hard to be brave.

My eyes looked round at familiar things we'd bought from year to year.
Three pictures from Switzerland;
There on the shelf stood two cow bells their tone I seemed to hear
As I touched them with my hand.

I smiled as I looked at all four walls each one a separate design.
We agreed to differ over this if I could paper the hall!
The years rolled backwards as I dreamed and lost all sense of time.
My mind thought I heard him call.

The mist of evening settled down and caressed his favourite chair.
Oh what was I going to do?
The room seemed suddenly warm to me and I felt his presence there.
The echo of past words came through.
'I shall know everything you do!'

Where there is love there is no parting.

A MODERN MIRACLE

The morning sky was a beautiful blue
With not a cloud in sight.
The drone of a plane could be heard there too,
The size determined its height.

It glided along towards the East
With its lights twinkling like stars.
A trail of vapour poured out behind
Making balls of fluff quite fast.

As I gazed at that plane my thoughts saw more
Than appeared to meet the eye.
For human souls were in control
Of that monstrous thing in the sky.

I prayed for their safety as it glided along,
Now a speck in the morning light.
The trails of soft balls were nearly all gone
As it disappeared from sight.

Those men up there were never aware
Of anyone thinking of them.
It was rather like the spiritual care
We can't see but know that God sends.

The progress of science makes us all think
Of the wonders around us each year.
Jesus walked on the water's brink.
Mankind choose to move in the air!